EXPLORATIONS

FINDING THE TITANIC

BY DALTON RAINS

WWW.APEXEDITIONS.COM

Apex is distributed by North Star Editions:
sales@northstareditions.com | 888-417-0195

Produced for Apex by Red Line Editorial.

Photographs ©: Christian Jegou/Science Source, cover; Shutterstock Images, 1, 4–5, 8–9, 14, 15, 22–23, 24–25, 27; Jim MacMillan/AP Images, 6–7, 29; Olivier Dugornay/IFREMER, 10–11; Bettmann/Getty Images, 12, 18–19; Mike Kullen/AP Images, 16–17; Xavier Desmier/Gamma-Rapho/Getty Images, 20–21, 26

Library of Congress Control Number: 2024941172

ISBN
979-8-89250-329-7 (hardcover)
979-8-89250-367-9 (paperback)
979-8-89250-440-9 (ebook pdf)
979-8-89250-405-8 (hosted ebook)

Printed in the United States of America
Mankato, MN
012025

NOTE TO PARENTS AND EDUCATORS

Apex books are designed to build literacy skills in striving readers. Exciting, high-interest content attracts and holds readers' attention. The text is carefully leveled to allow students to achieve success quickly. Additional features, such as bolded glossary words for difficult terms, help build comprehension.

TABLE OF CONTENTS

CHAPTER 1

FAMOUS SHIPWRECK

The *Titanic* was a huge passenger ship. It sank in 1912. People searched for the wreck for 70 years. But no one could find it.

The *Titanic* was one of the biggest, fanciest ships in the world. It carried more than 2,000 people.

SECRET SEARCH

The US Navy helped fund the search. But Navy leaders had a secret goal. They wanted to find sunken **submarines**. Looking for the *Titanic* was a cover. They didn't expect to actually find it.

In the 1980s, French and American scientists teamed up to search. Their leaders were Robert Ballard and Jean-Louis Michel. They planned to use **submersibles**.

Robert Ballard was an American scientist.

HOLE OCEANOGRAPHIC INSTITUTION
1930
OPERATION
TITANIC
OPERATION TITANIC

The scientists studied the ship's history. They tried to figure out where it likely sank. They **identified** an area of 100 square miles (260 sq km).

The *Titanic* hit an iceberg late at night on April 14, 1912. It sank into the Atlantic Ocean about three hours later.

FAST FACT

The *Titanic* sank while traveling from England to New York.

CHAPTER 2

TWO-PART SEARCH

The search began on July 1, 1985. First, French scientists used a ship called *Le Suroit.* It used **sonar**. It scanned the seafloor for several weeks. But it didn't find anything.

Le Suroit pulled a sonar system called SAR.

DSL

About 20 percent of the search area remained. An American ship called the *Knorr* took over. It pulled two submersibles. One was called ANGUS. The other was *Argo*.

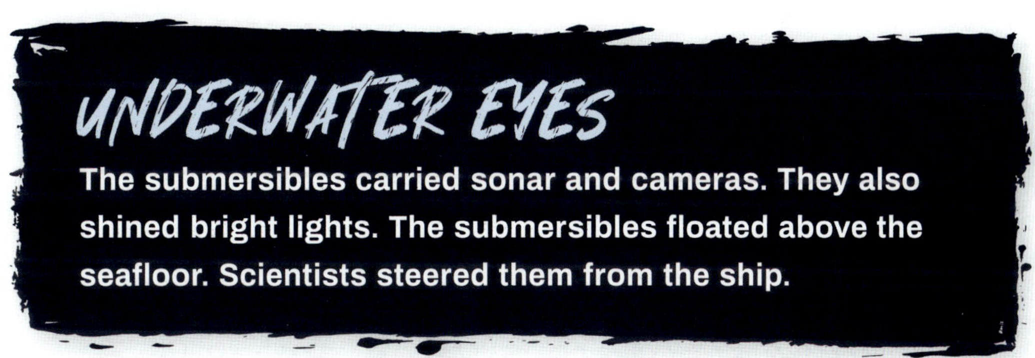

UNDERWATER EYES

The submersibles carried sonar and cameras. They also shined bright lights. The submersibles floated above the seafloor. Scientists steered them from the ship.

Argo was 15 feet (4.6 m) long. Its cameras sent black-and-white images to screens on the ship.

The *Titanic* had 29 giant boilers. They produced the steam that powered the ship.

The submersibles found the *Titanic*'s boilers on September 1. A trail of **debris** led to the rest of the ship.

FAST FACT

The *Titanic* was about 12,500 feet (3,810 m) below the surface.

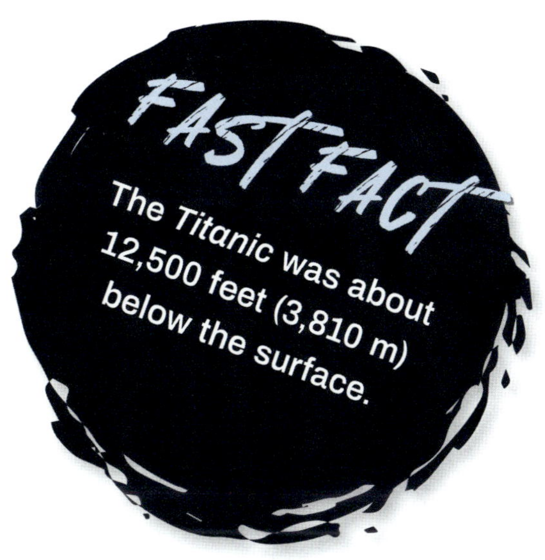

Ballard's team found the *Titanic* a few hundred miles from Newfoundland, Canada.

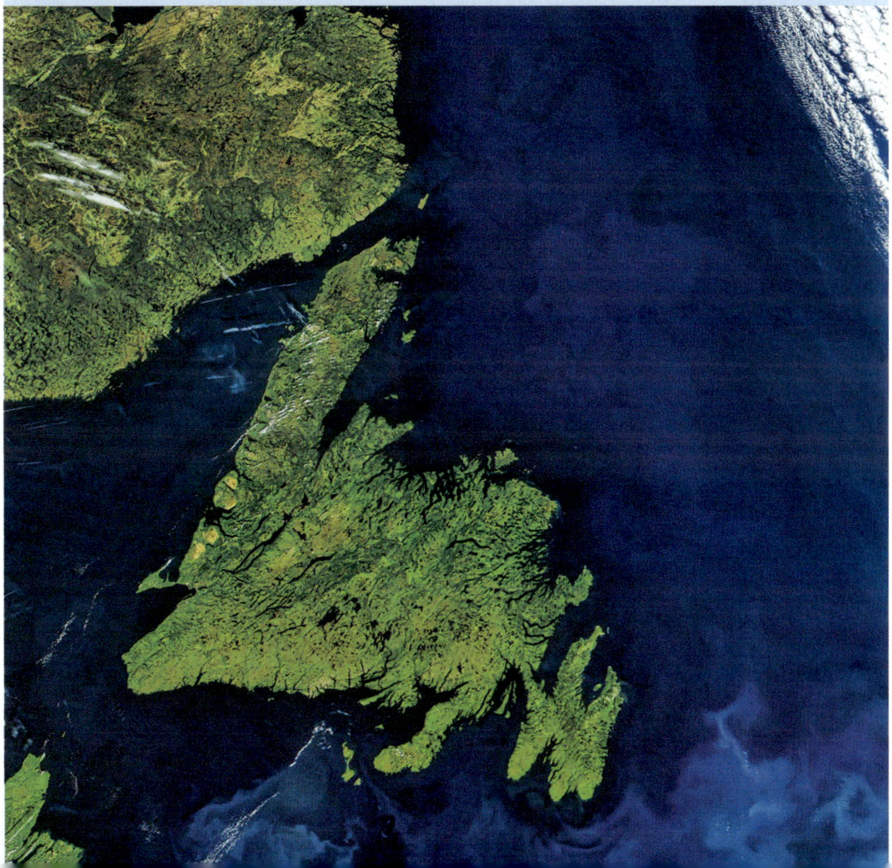

CHAPTER 3

RETURN TRIP

Ballard wanted to explore the wreck more. So, he went back in July 1986. This time, he used a submersible called *Alvin*. It could carry three people.

Ballard became famous after finding the *Titanic*.

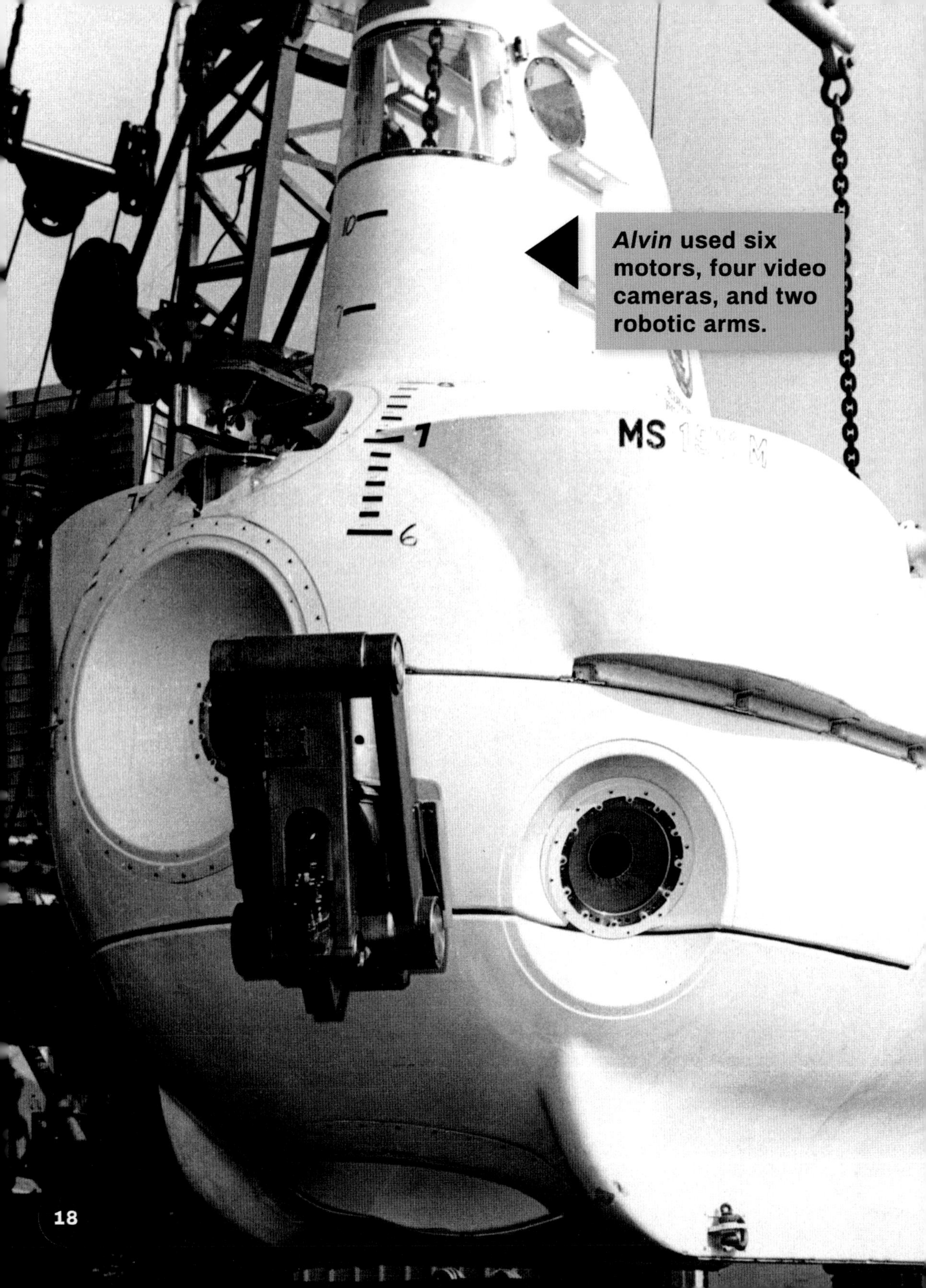

Alvin used six motors, four video cameras, and two robotic arms.

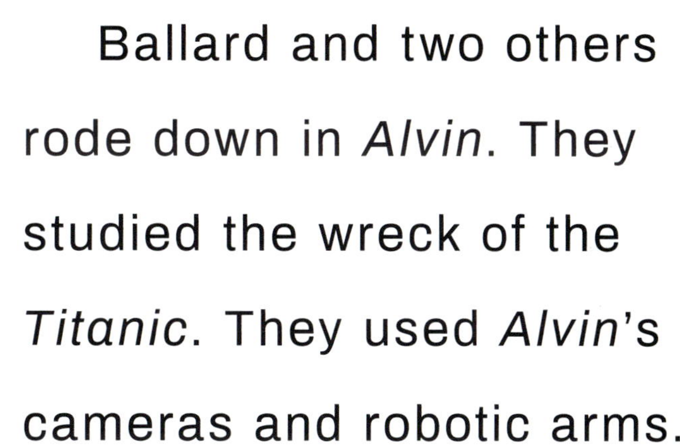

Ballard and two others rode down in *Alvin*. They studied the wreck of the *Titanic*. They used *Alvin*'s cameras and robotic arms.

DEEP DIVE

Alvin can go more than 14,000 feet (4,300 m) underwater. Most dives last eight hours. Going down takes two hours. So does coming back up. Four hours are spent working.

Studying parts of the wreck helped scientists learn how and why the ship sank.

The scientists took many photos and videos. They visited the ship's rooms. A smaller submersible went to areas that *Alvin* couldn't reach.

FAST FACT

The smaller submersible was called Jason Jr. A 300-foot (91-m) cable connected it to Alvin.

CHAPTER 4

LATER WORK

Other submersibles visited the wreck after that. Some carried scientists. For example, Ballard went back in 2004. Others brought tourists.

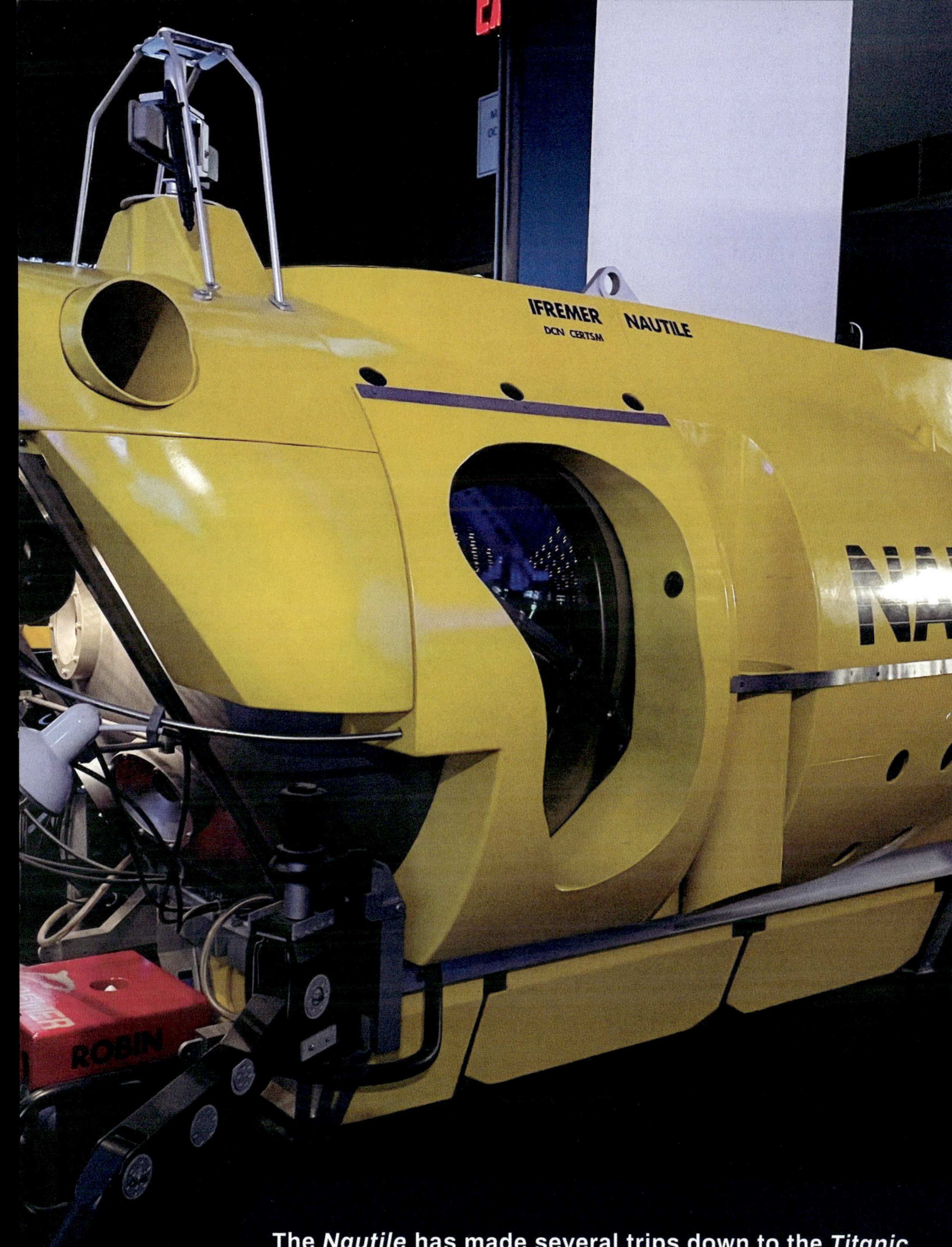

The *Nautile* has made several trips down to the *Titanic*.

People also collected **artifacts** from the ship. They brought thousands of items to the surface.

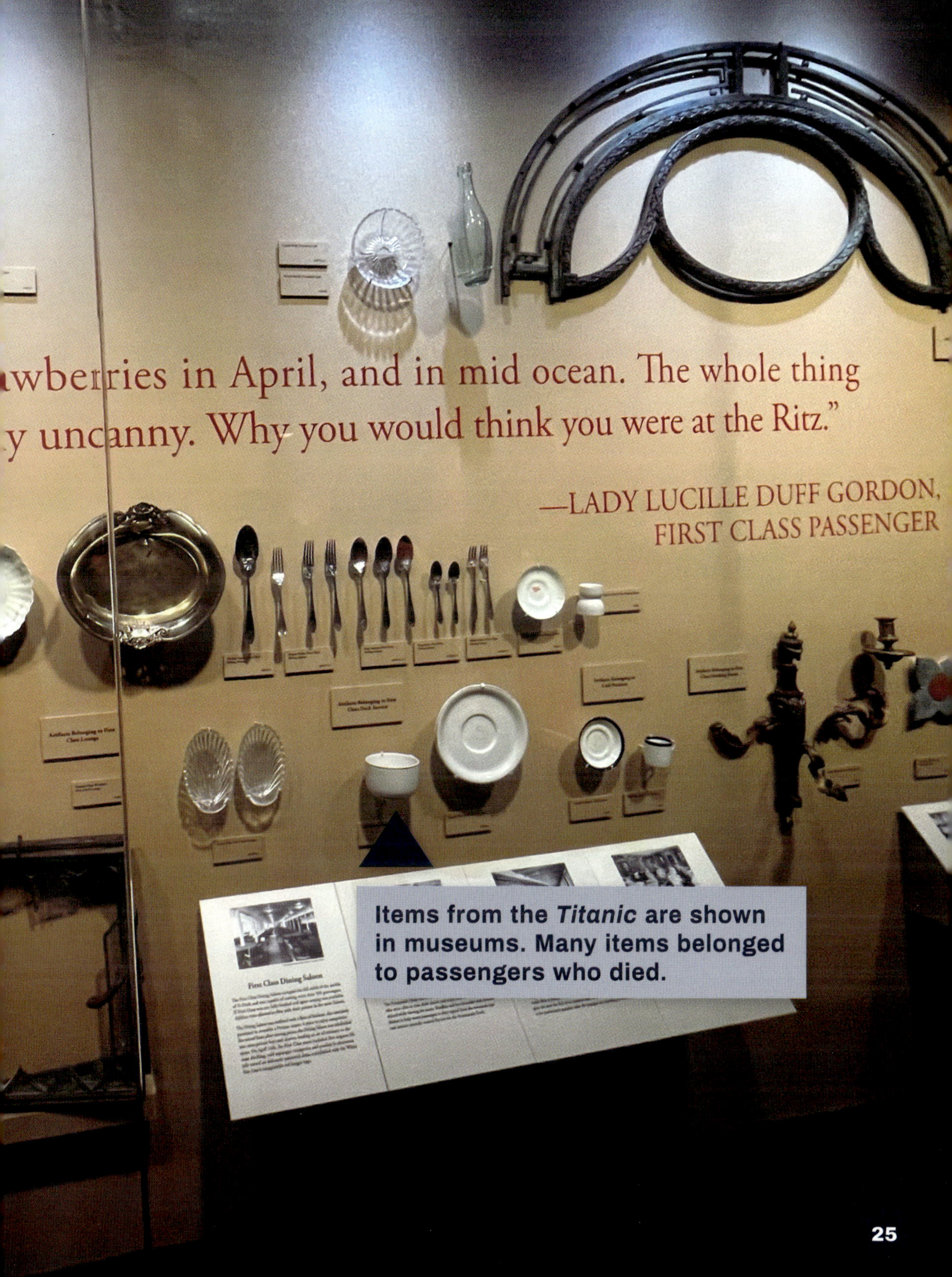

Items from the *Titanic* are shown in museums. Many items belonged to passengers who died.

The bacteria growing on the *Titanic* form strands that hang from the ship. Scientists call them "rusticles."

However, **bacteria** are growing on the *Titanic*. They cover it with fuzzy, icicle-like shapes. And they slowly eat the metal. By the 2020s, much of the ship was gone.

RISKY JOURNEY

People can pay to visit the *Titanic*. But the trip is very dangerous. The deep water has high **pressure**. In 2023, one submersible was crushed during a dive. Five people died.

Some museums have models of the *Titanic*. They show visitors what the wreck looks like.

COMPREHENSION QUESTIONS

Write your answers on a separate piece of paper.

1. Write a few sentences describing the main ideas of Chapter 2.

2. Would you want to visit the *Titanic* wreck? Why or why not?

3. Which submersible carried people down to the *Titanic*?

- **A.** ANGUS
- **B.** *Argo*
- **C.** *Alvin*

4. Why would water with high pressure be dangerous?

- **A.** It can speed things up.
- **B.** It can slow things down.
- **C.** It can crush things.

5. What does **cover** mean in this book?

But Navy leaders had a secret goal. They wanted to find sunken submarines. Looking for the Titanic *was a* ***cover****.*

A. a fake story

B. a sunken ship

C. a large blanket

6. What does **explore** mean in this book?

Ballard wanted to ***explore*** *the wreck more. So, he went back in July 1986.*

A. to hide from

B. to leave behind

C. to look at and study

Answer key on page 32.

GLOSSARY

artifacts
Objects made by humans in the past.

bacteria
Tiny living things.

debris
Pieces of something that broke or fell apart.

identified
Found or figured something out.

pressure
A force that pushes against something.

sonar
A system that uses sound waves to measure distances and find objects underwater.

submarines
Ships that can stay deep underwater for a long time.

submersibles
Small vehicles that move underwater and are often controlled from above the surface.

BOOKS

Murray, Julie. *Titanic*. Minneapolis: Abdo Publishing, 2024.

Oachs, Emily Rose. *Titanic*. Minneapolis: Bellwether Media, 2020.

Parkin, Michelle. *Atlantic Ocean Shipwrecks.* Minneapolis: Jump! Inc., 2024.

ONLINE RESOURCES

Visit **www.apexeditions.com** to find links and resources related to this title.

ABOUT THE AUTHOR

Dalton Rains is an author and editor from Saint Paul, Minnesota.

INDEX

ANSWER KEY:
1. Answers will vary; 2. Answers will vary; 3. C; 4. C; 5. A; 6. C